10 Baskets

of Biscuits

A Southern Counting Book

Written by Kelly Kazek

Illustrated by Michelle Hazelwood Hyde

Visit us at **southernthing.com**

Printed in Canada

First edition April 2021

ISBN: 978-1-57571-994-8 (hardback)

The night before visiting Grandma,

Charley couldn't close her eyes.

She was just too excited

And full of butterflies.

Mom said, "Try the counting game,

But instead of counting sheep,

Count things you'll see at
Grandma's house.

That should help you sleep."

Charley pulled the covers up

As mom tucked her into bed,

And thought of things at
Grandma's house

As she counted in her head.

1

One big Grandma kiss
And one big Grandma hug
That smelled like biscuits
And felt like love.

2

Two flower beds
Grandma planted from seeds
Sometimes Charley helped
By pulling up weeds.

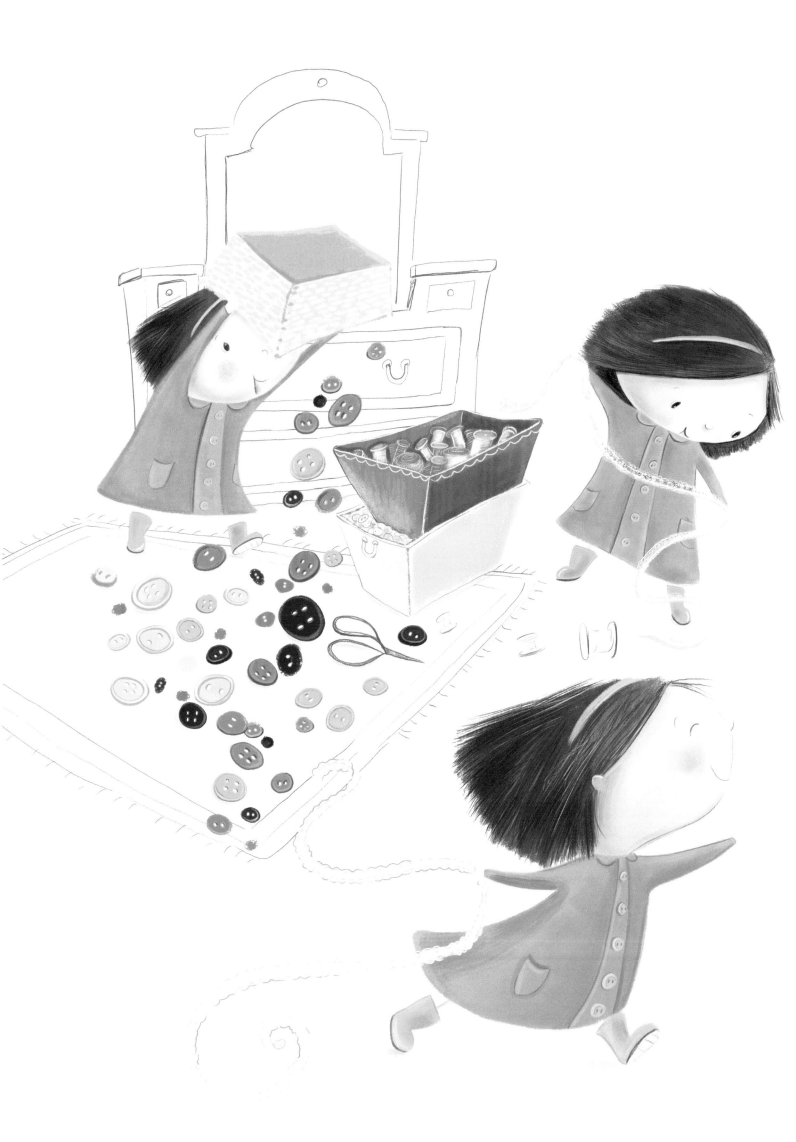

3

Three boxes of buttons

And bits of old lace

That Grandma collected

She said, "Just in case."

4

Four kinds of hard candies

In old-fashioned dishes

That Grandma refilled

Before every Christmas.

Five neighbor kids

Who all came to visit

Just to eat up

Grandma's buttermilk biscuits.

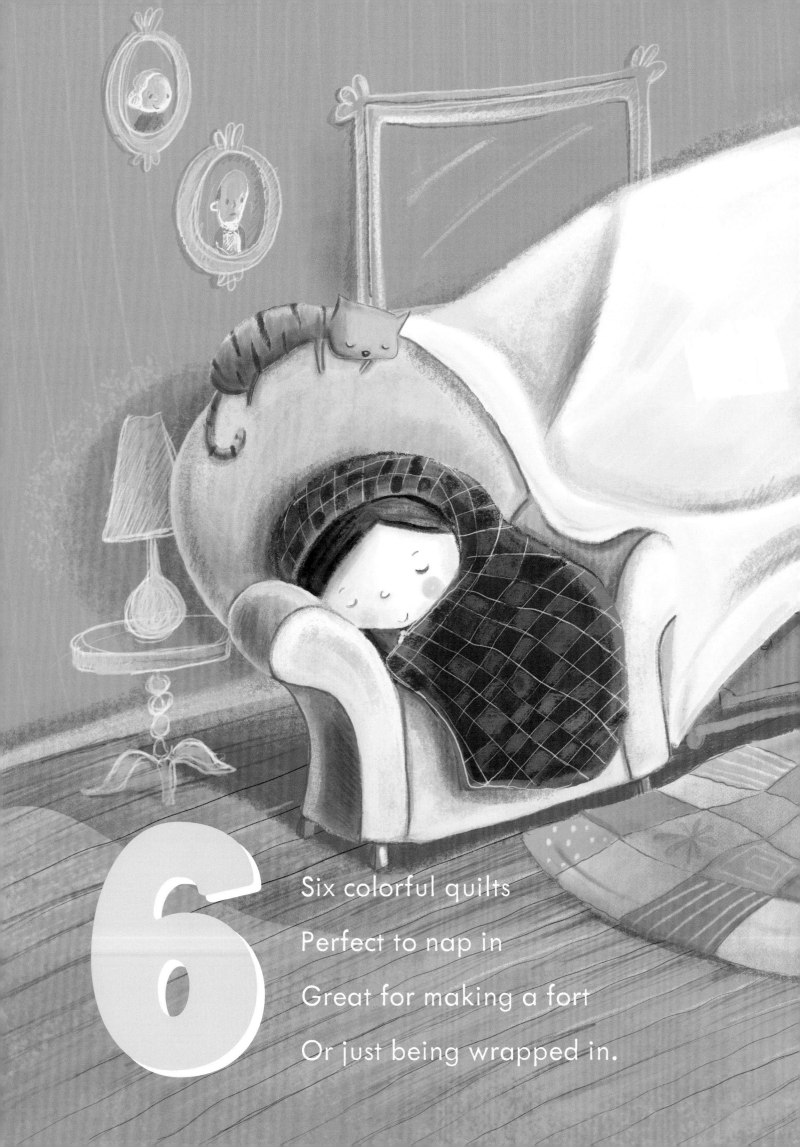

6

Six colorful quilts

Perfect to nap in

Great for making a fort

Or just being wrapped in.

7

Seven pecan pies

So very yummy

In Charley's mouth

And in her tummy.

8

Eight trees that grow peaches

To pick by the dozens

To make peach ice cream

To share with her cousins.

9

Nine collectible figures
Of little gnomes and elves
Arranged like a family
Upon Grandma's shelves.

Ten baskets of biscuits

Warm from the oven

Homemade by Grandma

With lots of loving.

Charley soon fell asleep,

Happy thoughts in her head.

She woke early the next day

And jumped from her bed.

At Grandma's house, Charley saw

All that she'd expected.

Quilts and candy, buttons and lace

And the figures Grandma collected.

When all the pies
were baked

And the ice cream had
been made,

Neighbors and
cousins

Came for pink
lemonade.

When it was time to leave,

Grandma was ready
with a hug.

She smelled a lot like biscuits

And felt a lot like love.

Also available from It's a Southern Thing:

Y is for Y'all

A Book of Southern ABCs

A Southern Night
Before Christmas

Visit store.southernthing.com *to buy yours!*